DAY ONE

New Woman

I love a good makeover story. You know the ones I'm talking about where someone goes in and has their hair, makeup, and wardrobe completely changed. In some instances, drastic weight loss happens. Those are my absolute favorites!

About 15 years ago, I weighed a good 80 pounds more than I do today and I truly didn't have any desire to change it. I ate a lot however I liked to eat so I was good, or so I thought. I went in for a physical and they proceeded to tell me that my cholesterol was extremely high and that I really needed to change some things.

I'm hardheaded so I went to a different doctor to get a second opinion.

Unfortunately, he said the same thing. Instead of taking medicine I set out to change myself through diet and exercise. It wasn't easy, but I began to see the hard work pay off. My clothes felt bigger and my energy had increased.

I felt like a NEW WOMAN!

A friend of mine that I hadn't seen in a couple of years came into town to visit. As soon as she saw me her response caught me off guard. She said, "I didn't recognize you! You look completely different!".

As Christ followers we are called to BE DIFFERENT. We are meant to be transformed from what we were into what He calls us to be.

Colossians 3:9-10 (ESV) 9 states that, "Do not lie to one another, seeing that you have put off the old self with its practices 10 and have put on the new self, which is being renewed in knowledge after the image of its creator".

2 Corinthians 5:17 (ESV) 17 says, "Therefore, if anyone is in Christ, he is a new creation. [a] The old has passed away; behold, the new has come. As soon as we accept Jesus as our personal savior, He sends us the Holy Spirit to guide and comfort us as we walk out this NEW LIFE! A change should occur - it HAS to. Jesus said that His followers would be known by the fruit they produce. It is the outcome of living a life following Him! The question today: Do you look different than you did before following Jesus? When someone sees you do, they see the OLD woman or the NEW?".

As soon as we accept Jesus as our personal savior, He sends us the Holy Spirit to guide and comfort us as we walk out into this NEW LIFE! When a change should occur - it HAS to. Jesus said that His followers would be known by the fruit they produce; It is the outcome of living a life following Him!

Question of the day: Do you look different than you did before following Jesus? When someone sees you, do they see the OLD or the NEW woman?

Galatians 5: 19-25 (ESV) 19 Now the works of the flesh are evident: sexual immorality, impurity, sensuality, 20 idolatry, sorcery, enmity, strife, jealousy, fits of anger, rivalries, dissensions, divisions,21envy, drunkenness, orgies, and things like these. I warn you, as I warned you before, that those who do such things will not inherit the kingdom of God. 22 But the fruit of the Spirit is love, joy, peace, patience, kindness, goodness, faithfulness, 23 gentleness, self-control; against such things there is no law. 24 And those who belong to Christ Jesus have crucified the flesh with its passions and desires.25 If we live by the Spirit, let us also keep in step with the Spirit.

DAY TWO

Lean in and listen

I love a good movie; One that has suspense, action, and a little bit of drama would be considered a top 10 on my list. However, there are specific scenes that seem to lose volume. You know what I'm talking about, those that are super loud in one scene then someone speaks in a whisper in the next scene. I have already turned down the volume because the action was so loud, but now I have found myself turning it up as high as it will go just to get some kind of idea of what was said. I will even pause and rewind to make sure I didn't miss anything. Isn't it funny how we will do things like that? However, when it comes to hearing from the Lord, we expect Him to yell, hit us over the head, or present it on a billboard?

1 Kings 19:20 (ESV) And after the earthquake a fire, but the LORD was not in the fire. And after the fire the sound of a low whisper. I feel like we spend so much time "asking of the Lord" but we really don't take the time to LEAN IN AND LISTEN.

How? I mean, we can't tangibly touch Him or see Him. So, how in the world would we hear Him? But we can! God uses His people to communicate to His people. He uses the surroundings, the radio, and sometimes, I have had Him use the TV!

Let me explain. I will pray for something of an answer, a piece of insight, or His wisdom, and a verse will either come to mind or I will somehow read over one. I would end prayer and then move on with my day, then out of NOWHERE that same verse would be spoken by a TV Evangelist, or in my situation, would be a topic on the morning talk radio! Some folks like to dismiss this as a "coincidence". However, with God there is no such thing as "coincidences". He is simply speaking to you. We just need to listen - then PROCLAIM!

Question of the day: Are you leaning in to listen?

Matthew 10:27 (ESV)What I tell you in the dark, speak in the light. What you hear in a whisper, proclaim on the housetops

DAY THREE

Pray and let it go

Oh, how I hate the phrase "Give it to God and let it go".

During the early phase in my Christian walk, I would hear this phrase all of the time. Unfortunately, no one ever took the time to truly explain what it meant or how it would be done. It became almost comical to me, like a catchphrase Christians used to dismiss someone going through those valleys of life.

I, like most people, have had my share of the valleys. During those tough times, nothing seemed to make sense no matter how much I tried. Me trying to "fix" the problem did not change my situation and, unfortunately, sometimes even made it worse. I would then pray and ask God to take it. I would read my bible looking for the "answer" by attending church and walking up to the altar for prayer...yet...nothing...changed!

Give it to God and let it go! What does that even mean Lord?! Here is the crazy thing - I couldn't find ONE VERSE that said "Give it to God and let it go" ... not ONE! However, there was a common thread through His word as I studied. 1 Peter 5:7 ESV Casting all your anxieties on him, because he cares for you. Psalm 55:22 (ESV) Cast your burden on the Lord, and he will sustain you; he will never permit the righteous to be moved. Philippians 4:19 (ESV) And my God will supply every need of yours according to his riches in glory in Christ Jesus.

Do you see what I see? It all comes down to taking Him at His word. I started to understand that as I "casted my anxieties onto

Him", then it was my responsibility to TRUST that He had them!

I began to put them into practice - I prayed over my situation and circumstances and told Him that I couldn't carry them anymore while asking (NO BEGGING) that He would take them. Then when I said AMEN, I had to trust He did. That meant that for EVERY time those thoughts would rise up "What am I going to do? How am I going to fix this? What is going to happen?", I would say - I have NO IDEA BUT God does, and His word says He cares for me, that He will sustain me and that He will supply my every need!

Question of the day: What are you still carrying that He has already taken? Romans 8:28 (ESV) And we know that for those who love God all things work together for good, for those who are called according to his purpose.

DAY FOUR

Trust fall

I know you've seen it, but have you ever done it? Stand on a high table or ladder and then fall into the arms of a group of people below? Why would anyone want to be a part of something like that? We don't even trust people enough to tell them our secrets much less trust them to save us from bodily harm! Yet, we are taught that by doing this type of exercise, because it builds a tighter bond within our group or team.

Trusting God is so much like the trust fall. We join His Team when we see that we are sinners in need of a savior and are ready to accept Christ. We completely trust Him to save us from the pits of hell, but do we trust Him in those everyday circumstances? When a co-worker makes us the topic of gossip or even worse, a family member or close friend spreads lies about us, do we trust that God will be there to protect us? I think our first reaction is anger, and what follows those flares of anger is usually a readiness to defend or attack. Yet, within God's word He says, Exodus 14:14 ESV, "The Lord will fight for you, and you have only to be silent".

We have a choice to make: Do we trust that HE WILL FIGHT, or do we dismiss it and rise up in rage? Do we let worry overtake us or even paralyze us, or can we trust that God will provide for our needs? Perhaps an unexpected bill comes due that is way more than we are able to pay. I'm not talking about a shopping spree but rather a true necessity that we just are not able to obtain on our own.

Philippians 4:6 (ESV) Do not be anxious about anything, but in every situation, by prayer and petition, with thanksgiving, present your requests to God.

The choice is ours - do we trust Him enough to not let the anxiety take over or do we worry ourselves into depression?

It is a TRUST FALL. The only difference is that the one catching us is the KING OF KINGS and LORD OF LORDS. He is our heavenly Father that loves us so much He sent His only son to die for us. His outcome is going to be so much better than anything we could come up with.

Question of the day: Are you ready to fall?

Isaiah 40:31 (ESV) But they who wait for the Lord shall renew their strength; they shall mount up with wings like eagles; they shall run and not be weary; they shall walk and not faint.

DAY FIVE

Journey = full life

Traveling is by far one of my most favorite things to do! I enjoy seeing new things and exploring new places. However, the time it takes to get there can be long depending on where I'm going.

Growing up my family and I would take yearly trips to Ft. Lauderdale each summer. I loved getting there and eating fresh mangos, spending days on the beach, and going shopping with my great grandmother who always knew how to have a good time. Yet the drive to get there would often take 12 hours! Spending over 12 hours in a car with your family with no room to stretch out and everyone arguing about what music to play or whether to turn the air conditioner up or down can really make it a miserable experience.

One year I decided that I wanted the entire time to be an adventure! I packed some items to keep me busy and made sure to take a blanket and pillow in the event I wanted to nap. I also made a map of items that I would try to spot on the way down in order to keep it interesting. By doing this, the journey down became almost as fun as the time I was there!

Life is the same way! If we have accepted Christ as our Savior then we are on a journey to Heaven! We have been promised an eternal home when this life on earth is finished, yet, we are living this journey like we are miserable.

John 10:10 (ESV) The thief comes only to steal and kill and destroy. I came that they may have life and have it abundantly.

Abundant (Greek definition): more than, beyond what is anticipated Christ came not only for us to experience and receive heaven when our lives are over.

He also came so that our lives on earth are FULL! Situations and circumstances WILL HAPPEN - there is no doubt!

Look what it says in Isaiah 43:2 (ESV) "When you pass through the waters, I will be with you; and through the rivers, they shall not overwhelm you; when you walk through fire you shall not be burned, and the flame shall not consume you".

Notice it says WHEN instead of IF. We will face hard things, however, our joy and peace are not defined or determined by those things. We are a light unto the world, a city on a hill, the hope for the hopeless - BECAUSE OF JESUS!

Question of the Day: How will YOU shine in your situations and circumstances today?

James 4:14 (ESV) yet you do not know what tomorrow will bring. What is your life? For you are a mist that appears for a little time and then vanishes.

DAY SIX

Faith Eyes

2 Corinthians 5:7 (ESV) For we walk by faith, not by sight.

One of the hardest things for me to do is to go somewhere without having any idea how to get there, in other words, I need a plan. There was a time that I carried a paper map in my car just in case I wandered outside my little neck of the woods (which was almost never).

As long as I stayed near home, a few simple directions could always get me where I needed to go. No map needed here. My husband thought he would broaden my horizons and move me an hour away from my little "neck of the woods". My outings became comical to say the least until I finally learned my way around. Yet, even with my newfound confidence I relied on Siri (and still do) quite a bit.

It's amazing to me how confident we are with our phone maps and the directions it gives us. We type in a destination all the way across the U.S. and we will follow it to a "T" with confidence of the time of our arrival.

What if we followed God the same way? We type in our destination (JOY, for instance) and then whatever His word has to say about getting to that destination, we have so much confidence that we follow it exactly the way He says.

Walking by faith and not by sight ... we have faith in so many things, yet HE is asking us to follow Him as closely as we do everything else, and then we flinch because we just aren't sure what the outcome will be. Yet He tells us in Romans 8:28 that all things work together for good … and that Phil 4:13 we can do all things through Jesus.

James 1:22 (ESV) But be doers of the word, and not hearers only, deceiving yourselves.

If we type in our destination into our "map app", and do not move, then we never get to where we are going. A life lived to the fullest trusting God with everything we have is the destination I want. I've typed it in and now it's time to follow.

Question of the day:
What do you need to follow that He has already told you? Psalm 128:1 (ESV) Blessed is everyone who fears the LORD, who walks in his ways!

DAY SEVEN

His Way

I am one of those people who has a list for everything: groceries, goals, to-dos. You name it, I have a list for it. Packing for a trip? Yep, a list. Going on vacation? I make a list that includes things to do along with must-see attractions. Don't even get me started on scheduling lists for my work, my kid's classes, and after school activities. It's bad, I know.

Another thing about me is how I stick to my lists. I like to be in control and know how long things will take. Imagine my surprise when I realized that God's way will not match my list, 9 out of 10 times? He and I have been around about the goals that I felt HE GAVE ME or the "to-dos" of the day that HE helped me plan and then things never turned out that way.

Why the change of direction, Lord? Why the interruptions on my way here or there?

The funny thing about God is that when we truly ask, He will answer. Jeremiah 29:13 "You will seek me and find me, when you seek me with all your heart".

The answer? The list, itinerary, goal was the end result. Who I was becoming on my way there was more important to God. The interruptions would teach me patience, the disasters would teach me peace, and the hurdles I would have to climb over to get there would teach me grace and mercy. At the end of life God doesn't care how many goals we have accomplished, how many titles we have, or how many degrees we have achieved. He wants to know how well we have loved others, and how well we showed the world around us who He truly is. Oh to hear those words "Well done good and faithful servant".

Question of the day: What is he teaching you through the interruptions today? Proverbs 16:9 The heart of man plans his way, but the LORD establishes his steps.

DAY EIGHT

Reap or Sow?

Opinions - we all have them. Unfortunately, some of us like to give ours even when no one really wants, or cares, to hear them. It seems the more we have an understanding about a subject or situation, the more we have a "right" to voice our opinion.

The question is: But do we?

Matthew 7:2 "For with the judgment you pronounce you will be judged, and with the measure you use it will be measured to you". We see here in Matthew that the standard we hold upon others will be the same we ourselves will be held to.

For some that may not be a big deal.

Someone would be like, "I'm good with that". My standards are high, and I hold myself to the same standard as I do everyone else!

But what if it is an "off" day when you aren't feeling well, or your emotions are all over the place? Then what do you do?

A few years ago, I used to travel and sing at various events, from gatherings to funerals to weddings and church services. I believed with everything in me that God was moving every time I yielded myself to Him as a tool to be used for His glory. HOWEVER, something shifted. The pats on the back became way more important than they should've, and I started thinking I was some sort of music connoisseur.

I began to critique others when I saw them perform. I would put my head down and cringe when they missed a note, or even snicker if I thought it was off pitch. The thing about the Lord is that if you truly desire to walk with Him HE WILL WHIP YOU when you act up. Ok, a better word might be DISCIPLINE; However, whatever you call it the Lord will put us in our place when we get too big for our britches.

It wasn't long after my critique session that I took the platform to perform. The music started and I proudly belted out the most terrible shriek you could imagine. I quickly stopped, took a breath, tried again. NOPE, same thing. The rest of the song I begged God to stop the madness and allowed them to hear Him instead of me. As the song ended and I went to my seat with utter shame written all over my face, He reminded me of something. Galatians 6:7 "Do not be deceived: God is not mocked, for whatever one sows, that will he also reap". It was His platform, NOT mine. He quickly reminded me and suddenly I felt the weight of all the judgment I had placed on those other performers now directed at me.

Question of the day: What are you reaping from what you sowed?

DAY NINE

Lesson or Blessing

What if every circumstance we encountered in life we saw as either a lesson or a blessing?

What if those people that drive us crazy and those situations that make us lose our minds are not just there to annoy us?

Imagine with how our experiences of life would change if we could see every encounter and circumstance as either (1) teaching us a lesson or (2) giving us a blessing.

Situation: You left for work right on time only to get stuck in traffic. Lesson or blessing? At the grocery store you don't notice that you forgot your wallet until the cashier tells you the total. Lesson or blessing? What if the person behind you pays for the groceries? Lesson or blessing? We hear that someone we love dearly is talking bad about us. Lesson or blessing?

Jesus used stories to teach those around Him. In each story we can see either a lesson or a blessing. I believe that our lives tell a story and each day is a new page. We certainly can't move forward by rereading the pages of yesterday, but we can take away a lesson or blessing as we reflect and move on to the page of today.

Sometimes we are fortunate enough to see both a lesson and a blessing. God uses everything. Nothing is wasted in our stories. Pain, laughter, hurt, and joy all have a purpose, and He uses them to mold us into who He created us to be.

I don't know about you, but I am so thankful that He is patient with me as I filter through my selfishness to see the true perspective of either a lesson or a blessing.

Question of the day: Are you experiencing a lesson or blessing in your current situation?

2 Corinthians 9:8 "And God is able to make all grace abound to you, so that having all sufficiency in all things at all times, you may abound in every good work".

DAY TEN

Pride

In 2 Chronicles chapter 26 we meet a king named Uzziah. Uzziah became King at the ripe old age of 16 and did well for the Lord. In the first 14 verses we see how God helps him defeat armies and build the kingdom strong, but then pride gets the best of Uzziah. He begins to take matters into his own hands thinking he knows best and he can rule in his own strength. I mean he is king after all!

There are certainly things the Lord dislikes, and then there are some that He just outright hates: Proverbs 6:16-19 "There are six things the Lord hates, seven that are detestable to him: haughty eyes, a lying tongue, hands that shed innocent blood, a heart that devises wicked schemes, feet that are quick to rush into evil, a false witness who pours out lies and a person who stirs up conflict in the community".

Proverbs 8:13 "The fear of the LORD is hatred of evil. Pride and arrogance and the way of evil and perverted speech I hate".

There are so many other verses in His word that cover pride and how it brings destruction.

King Uzziah learned firsthand how destructive pride can be. After seeing how powerful he had become, King Uzziah decided to take matters into his own hands, and I have to admit, so have I ... too many times to count.

We can see that Pride is not a laughing matter to God. So how do we know if we are a prideful person? Why, I'm glad you asked.

Here are a few statements that are a key indicator you may have a pride problem:

1. Do you look down on those who are less educated, less affluent, less refined, or less successful than yourself?

2. Do you think of yourself as more spiritual than your mate or others in your church?

3. Do you have a judgmental spirit toward those who don't make the same lifestyle choices you do in terms of dress standards, how you school your kids, entertainment standards, etc.?

4. Do you have a sharp, critical tongue?

5. Do you frequently correct or criticize your mate, your pastor, or other people in positions of leadership (teachers, youth director, etc.)?

6. Do you frequently interrupt people when they are speaking?

Eye opening isn't it? Pride brings destruction and always brings a fall.

Question of the day: In what area of your life are you prideful?

DAY ELEVEN

Battlefield

Have you ever felt misunderstood? Some days no matter how you say or convey it, it could seem like you are speaking a whole different language.

I recently had a conversation in which no matter how hard I tried, the other person would not or could not receive it the way I originally intended. No matter how I changed my wording, the inflections in my voice or my body language, the message was misunderstood. I finally realized that removing myself from the conversation was the best option, however, when I did my heart fell to pieces.

Why?

Because strife and dissension are not of God and I want more than anything to follow Him. I felt like I had just left a boxing ring where blow after blow came and nothing I could do or say had any effect. I was mentally and physically drained. Yet, I never left my couch. I was sitting the entire time. That is exactly why we must understand the TRUE battle we are in.

Ephesians 6:12 "For we do not wrestle against flesh and blood, but against the rulers, against the authorities, against the cosmic powers over this present darkness, against the spiritual forces of evil in the heavenly places".

The people around us aren't our enemy. They can be used by the enemy, but they aren't the enemy! Now, don't get all self-right-eous because he uses you, and I sometimes too. None of us are immune from falling prey to the enemy's ways.

I dare say that many times we are even unaware that we are being used. Satan knows exactly what will set us up and set us off. He manipulates the circumstances around us and uses those areas where we struggle the most to make us slip.

Why?

We love Jesus and the Holy Spirit lives within us! Satan knows he can't win! Why would he go through all the trouble if he knew he couldn't?

When the enemy can't get into a situation, he will use a bitter Christian to do it for him. It makes us look hypocritical, judgmental, and no different from the world if he can get us to act just like those who don't love Jesus! Why would I want to follow Christ when those that do show anything but LOVE? Why would I want to go to church with people that act one way on Sunday and completely different through the week?

I have heard it said, "Many in church today are Sunday warriors and then Monday whiners."
YIKES! So, what on earth do we do?

In the boxing ring, remember who we are fighting! Remember that God has called us to LOVE above all else. The situation may mean that you have to bow out, regroup, take a breather in the corner ... go back in the fight? Yes, but this time is should look a whole lot different!

First, pray for a heart that is right, a spirit humble enough to see and own up to mistakes made, and the self-control necessary to avoid hurling insults or taking insults hurled to heart.

Second, pray for the other person. Genuinely pray for them, not through gritted teeth but truly seeking peace. Pray for blessings on them.

Finally, go back in love, admitting where you were wrong or came across in a way that wasn't the best - and say nothing else!

Don't try to prove any points, don't try to look more spiritual, and don't try to have the upper hand. Just leave it at "I'm sorry, that wasn't my intention."

The battle WILL change! You WILL WIN. Maybe the circumstance won't change, BUT YOU WILL and that's all we should be concerned about anyway. He wants us to be more like Him - to be moldable and teachable. He cares way more about who we are becoming than where we are going.

Question of the day: Who is someone that you may need to apologize to? A situation that you need to own up to? He is already showing you right now - follow Him!

DAY TWELVE

It Works

I got a wild hair and decided to cut the grass for my husband before he got home! I was thrilled once the idea came, however, the excitement dwindled quickly as it began to sink in that I would actually have to get up and go out to do it. Nonetheless, I got up and did it.

I ventured out to the shed and unlocked the door. As I opened it a feeling of, "I am woman hear me roar!" came over me and I got a surge of energy! I pulled the lawnmower out ready to conquer the yard when all of a sudden, I was puzzled!

The lawnmower did not crank the way I had thought it would as I jerked at it with all my might. Of course, this was a gradual build up just in case anyone that might be watching wouldn't think that I wasn't strong enough or didn't know what I was doing. No matter how I tried, the cord would not move! I knew the machine was a bit old and that it was "special" but seriously how "special" was it? I did not want to call my husband! Yet I was getting nowhere so I had to give in and call. As he talks me through how to crank this pitiful machine, I hung up laughing so hard. His instructions: "Do you see the string on the left side?" That cable is broken so you will need to attach that string around the front of the mower. It is just the right length!" He said this almost proud of himself. Then he proceeded to tell me to "prime" it which wasn't that bad. However, right before hanging up he said, "Do you see the bungee cord attached to the handle?" I looked and shook my head in disbelief, "Yes." He instructed, "Be sure that when the mower bogs down that you pull that so the grass can clean out!" SERIOUSLY? I laughed so hard as I hung up the phone. His response was a simple text back that said, "it works!" Yes, it did! It cut the entire yard and was still ready for more. It reminded me of us. We get worn down by life. We even get broken in areas that never seem to heal. Yet God has created us FOR A PURPOSE! As long as we follow Him – NOTHING can stand in the way! We may have to get creative in how we adapt, but we will always OVERCOME!

Romans 8: 37 No, in all these things we are more than conquerors through him who loved us. 38 For I am sure that neither death nor life, nor angels nor rulers, nor things present nor things to come, nor powers, 39 nor height nor depth, nor anything else in all creation, will be able to separate us from the love of God in Christ Jesus our Lord.

Question of the day: What is it that you need to PUSH through today?

Remember - He has you!

DAY THIRTEEN

Don't Give Up

Recently I noticed the "reduced" area in the garden section at our local hardware store. It was a rack of wilted plants with some even brown and dried. They were originally priced anywhere from $15.00 to $20.00 and now marked down to $1.00! I glanced over at the pitiful looking items and thought, "I wouldn't give a penny much less a 1.00!" When I saw an older lady pulling the very ones I looked over into her cart, I couldn't help but ask, "did you find a deal?", and she replied, "Oh my yes!" with the proudest smile on her sweet face. I responded, "Really? They all seem dead to me!", and she simply responded with, "it's all in how you look at them. When YOU look you see brown leaves and dry soil. When I look and see the tiny bit of green still left on the leaf and know that I have water!".

What a lesson friends! It makes me think of those situations and even people around us that we may give up on! Maybe if we change the way we SEE them, we can see a tiny bit of life. Nowadays we are so quick to give up. We give up on jobs, relationships, churches, and people in general.

What if HE gave up on us? Lord knows that He could have given up on me many times. I think back to my life before Him and I can see how far He has brought me. What about you? Perspective is something we all have. Would you define your perspective as an optimistic or pessimistic one? As Christ followers I believe we are to always be optimistic! I mean even if the worst thing I could imagine happens, He would still win in the end and I would still be with Him. One of my most favorite verses is Isaiah 43:2, "When you pass through the waters, I will be with you; and through the rivers, they shall not overwhelm you; when you walk through fire you shall not be burned, and the flame shall not consume you". I am so glad that when I fall, He picks me back up. When I mess up, He guides me to how to fix it. When I slip, He catches me. And, no matter what, He never gives up! From knowing these things, when I look through the lens of Christ, I should see things and people differently. I should see them the way He does. So, when I feel like giving up, I may just need to change my perspective.

"Don't Quit."

When things go wrong, and they sometimes will, when the road you're trudging seems all uphill, when the funds are low and the debts are high, and you want to smile, but you have to sigh, when care is pressing you down a bit, rest, if you must, but don't you quit. Life is queer with its twists and turns, as every one of us sometimes learns, and many a failure turns about, when he might have won had he stuck it out; Don't give up though the pace seems slow – You may succeed with another blow. Often the goal is nearer than It seems to a faint and faltering man, often the struggler has given up, when he might have captured the victor's cup, and he learned too late when the night slipped down, how close he was to the golden crown. Success is failure turned inside out – The silver tint of the clouds of doubt, And you never can tell how close you are, It may be near when it seems so far, So stick to the fight when you're hardest hit– It's when things seem worst that you mustn't quit. - Author Unknown.

It's in our weakness that He is strong!

Question of the day: What is it that you thought was over that He is asking you to not give up on?

DAY FOURTEEN

Breath of Life

In Genesis 2:7 the bible says that God breathed the breath of life into Adam. Have you ever thought about that moment? Have you pictured it in your mind's eye? As the water from the earth mixed with the dust to form the clay, God himself formed and shaped Adam's body, so carefully crafting every last detail. I imagined Him getting up close to create each intricate part — eyelids, fingernails, the shape of the ears. As He steps back to take a look at His creation (as artists do), He knows it is almost complete. One final touch. At the right moment…the perfect one…He kneels down to breathe into Adam's nostrils. Watching as Adam's chest rise and color comes to his skin. WOW!!!! It gets me every time! Why? Because He did the same for each of us! Did you know that?

As we were being formed in the womb, HE FORMED US! For you formed my inward parts; Psalm 139 you knitted me together in my mother's womb. 14 I praise you, for I am fearfully and wonderfully made. [a] Wonderful are your works; my soul knows it very well. 15 My frame was not hidden from you, when I was being made in secret, intricately woven in the depths of the earth. 16 Your eyes saw my unformed substance; in your book were written, every one of them, the days that were formed for me, when as yet there was none of them. He put together every part of you, paying attention to every detail of who you are. NOTHING is by accident and NOTHING is by mistake! Then as soon as you passed through the birth canal – HE BREATHED INTO YOUR NOSTRILS! Research shows that within 10 seconds of a baby being born the first breath is taken by the lungs and then so many other things are happening all at once for their little bodies to adjust and adapt...and...HE CREATED US TO DO IT! HE made us JUST the way we are then HE breathed LIFE into us. Curly hair, straight hair, brown skin, olive skin, tall, short...we are made in HIS image – PERFECT!

Still, we so easily get caught up in wanting better or different, don't we? Looking over at her nice toned skin and gorgeous eyes or his ability to play basketball, we begin to wish we looked like them or had a talent or ability just like them. We forget that He shaped and molded and BREATHED life into us. Let's not compare ourselves to those around us but instead BE FREE TO BE who HE created US TO BE!

Question of the day: Who or what are you comparing yourself to?

"A flower never compares itself to the other flowers around it, it just blooms where it's planted". It's time to BLOOM.

DAY FIFTEEN

The "IN" crowd

I think we all want to be IN. Being "out" would mean that we wouldn't measure up or make the cut. It's like not being picked or worse being picked last for a pickup game of basketball. We feel like we have failed, but we are not really sure what we failed to do or not do to make us OUT instead of IN. We don't understand the reasons why or how to fix them. We remember those years in middle and high school when we were either IN or OUT, and some of us were so thankful when it was finally OVER. But is it really over?

Do you still sometimes look around at different groups and wonder "why didn't they ask me?". A group of friends would go out and the only reason you know about it is because you caught the social media feed. Your boss overlooks you for a job promotion. You aren't invited to a party. You are left feeling inadequate and unaccepted, just like when you were in Middle and High school. It's so funny how the enemy will reel us back in. How he uses our INsecurities to send us down a road that I can almost promise is imaginary. The emotions run wild inside of us, yet the reality is that GOD didn't plan for us to be there! If He did, then we would be. Seriously! Don't we see that HE is greater? So, if He wanted us to be IN that group that went out or have that job promotion or go to that party, then WE WOULD BE.

His plans are to prosper us, not harm us. His ways are higher than ours. God created us to stand OUT! He created us each with a different perspective, a different look and placed us in a different group so that WE COULD MAKE AN IMPACT.

The place we are in right this very second is one that HE can use. The people that are around us, HE PLACED THEM THERE! Nothing is just a coincidence! He may have left you OUT to remind you to stand OUT. Do NOT to let your INsecurities drive you to be IN. In HIS Kingdom, if you have accepted Jesus – you are IN!

Question of the Day: What can you do to stand OUT for Jesus today?

DAY SIXTEEN

Open Door

Mornings are my favorite times to sit and reflect. It is when the house is quiet, the rays of the sun are just barely peeking through the blinds and the smell of coffee brewing fills the room. I love to sit in a special spot while looking out the glass storm door.

One morning while deep in thought and prayer, that same storm door decided to open by itself! It caught me completely off guard as I continued to sit there and try to figure out exactly how and why it happened. I began to slowly get up to close it because let me be frank, I WAS SLIGHTLY AFRAID! My mind was going through a million suggestions as I sat still not able to get up and close the door. I laughed to myself as I went back to sitting space, when all of a sudden, it hit me! I have prayed for doors to open and close so many times in my life and for God to show me clearly the direction to take. However, how many times has the door opened and reason the HOW and WHY instead of just going through it?

We go through the, "It's not possible", or, "It's too good to be true", or, "I don't have enough, education, money, self-esteem, and so on...". We forget that God is all about the IMPOSSIBLES. Jesus said, Matthew 19:26 (ESV) "With man this is impossible, but with God all things are possible." However, like my storm door, we tend to stop in our tracks and second guess why we should TRUST HIM. BUT, how do you know the door open is the one from Him? I mean, let's be real - not all of them are. The enemy would love nothing more than to take us through a door that points AWAY from God.

We have to stay in prayer, know what His word says (He will NEVER contradict His word), and believe it must take us to lean on Him. If it's something we can do with our eyes closed, it's more than likely NOT HIM. God's desire is for us to walk closely with Him, lean and trust the entire time all while remembering WE ARE NOTHING WITHOUT HIM.

Question of the day: What door is He opening that you aren't trusting and leaning on Him to walk through?

DAY SEVENTEEN

Waiting

Patience is one of those words I don't think I ever understood. Even when I had been walking with the Lord for a while, I always thought it was just, "waiting for something to come to fruition". God has a way of enlightening us if we would just take the time to lean into Him and listen. What does THAT mean? I have come to the realization that most of my time spent feeling aggravated, irritated and impatient is the very moment He is trying to show me something.

Waiting has come to be the very times I have learned the most. Patience is actually, "having the right attitude IN the waiting". It's changing the focus off what my desire is and instead seeing a bigger picture of what His desire is. It's in the waiting time that we have no control. We can't hurry it up or make things change when we want them to. We have an amusement park fairly close to us that we have the opportunity to go to. As we are on the drive, however, we must endure a lot of traffic. No matter what time we leave, cars are packed on the interstate like sardines and there is nothing we can do to hurry the process!

We simply have to wait. Its during one of these moments that I specifically feel the Lords nudge. Our car had a few kids that were so excited and let's face it, so was I. The anticipation was building but while we sat in the traffic frustration began and built with each passing second. I felt my heart rate pick up and then had the bright idea to change lanes in one of those aggressive movements. I turned the wheel a little too quickly and almost side swiped the vehicle beside me. The anger grew when all of a sudden, I took a deep breath and looked around at the scenery. I began to notice most of the folks in the other cars were having the same type of experience. I heard this small calm voice say, "If you have a wreck then you will not get to the park at all". That same voice spoke again, "Life is too short to live it in this state of mind". I looked around in the car at the sad faces around me, then had an idea! We turned the music up and began to play, "What's the name of this song". The drive slowly became just part of the journey to enjoy.

There is something to be said for the journey. Let's face it, we will have MANY lines that we will be in throughout our lives. According to a "Timex Survey", Americans spend an average of 6 months of their lives in lines waiting. When you compare that to the average length of life expectancy of, which is 71.5 years, you have to wonder why we get so upset. The reality is this, even if our waiting time was longer, there is nothing we can do about it. So, why not take a look at it in a different way? He may be trying to get our attention and its only in the waiting that we will see it and learn.

Question of the day: What is He showing you while you wait? Lamentations 3:25 (ESV) - The Lord is good to those who wait for Him, to the soul who seeks Him.

DAY EIGHTEEN

Impressions

Have you ever left a conversation and second guessed yourself? Did the thoughts, "Did I talk to much?", or, "Was I too loud?", or, "Did I seem overbearing?", or, "Do they even like me?", go through your mind? For the longest time, I would do this way more than I'd like to admit. I had a huge desire to be accepted and be liked that I would try to impress those I would be around.

The problem is, whatever you use or become to do the "impressing", you have to be able to keep it going to maintain it. In simple terms - Following Jesus can be challenging. Choosing His way is always the right way but hardly ever is it the easy way. Galatians 1:10 (ESV) "For am I seeking the approval of man, or of God? Or am I trying to please man?". If I was still trying to please man, I would not be a servant of Christ.

He hit me square in the face one day with this scripture. I desperately wanted to follow Jesus and earn His acceptance. If that is indeed the truth, then something had to shift! I had to get to a point of being who He created me to be and walk in the confidence of that.

That meant letting go of what other people thought or felt about me. Of course we want friends, right? We want that promotion in our jobs, the raise around the corner, to be a part of the team! Here is what I have learned - whatever we "become" to get that promotion, gain that next friend, obtain that raise or be a part of that team, we will have to continue to maintain in order to keep it. Talk about exhausting! We have to remember that everything we do in our lives has got to be based on truth. That truth, the core of who we are, is how we become who Christ intended for us to be. He is always looking at our hearts.

1 Samuel 16:7 (ESV) But the Lord said to Samuel, "Do not look on his appearance or on the height of his stature, because I have rejected him. For the Lord sees not as a man sees; man looks on the outward appearance, but the Lord looks on the heart". It doesn't matter who we try to be, but our motives have to be true and pure. If not, the people around us may be impressed for a moment but then slowly, with each passing "impression", we would begin to lose our identity.

Question of the Day: Who are you trying to impress today?

DAY NINETEEN

Chips and Peels

Fingernails have become somewhat of an art form. There are a variety of crazy designs that even include gluing gems on them to give an extra bling. I will admit, from time to time I would get wrapped up in it. However, I'm usually the girl that clear polish is about all I can deal with. Why? Because one chip or peel on them causes my OCD to kick in and then I would get distracted from everything else until it would get fixed!

I am so bad that I will carry the nail color in my purse "just in case" a chip occurs so that I could touch it up until I had the time to redo them all! Recently, it hit me that life is a lot like those nails. We get a chip, make a mistake or fall short, instead of getting to the bottom of it and allowing His Holy Spirit to start us all over, we just add another layer of polish to cover it up. Have you ever noticed that the more polish you add to the chip, the more you are able to notice the imperfections? Sometimes stripping it all off and starting over would take more work, but the finished product is immeasurably different.

Lamentations 3:22-23 (ESV), "The steadfast love of the Lord never ceases; his mercies never come to an end; they are new every morning; great is your faithfulness".

Our mess ups, mistakes, and bad judgements never have to be covered up when we follow Jesus! When we fall at his feet and allow him to strip away all of those things that are not of Him, he starts us over. Actually, it's only at that point when He is able to work far beyond what we could even comprehend. Not showing our chips has become the norm. Not allowing others to see the areas where we fall short, however, Paul the apostle was reminded by the Lord.

2 Corinthians 12:9 (ESV), But he said to me, "My grace is sufficient for you, for my power is made perfect in your weakness". Therefore, I will boast all the more gladly of my weakness, so that the power of Christ may rest on me. Following Jesus is so different than today's world's view, because the world tells us to hide the flaws whether it be nails, hiding the gray in our hair, cream to cover the wrinkles. On the other hand, Jesus tells us to embrace them all because it's in those weakness that He will shine the brightest.

Question of the day: What weakness are you trying to cover up that He wants to use to shine?

DAY TWENTY

Change

A few years ago, I was told that I needed to work on my health issues (you have to know me in order to understand why this was an issue). You see, I like to eat and not only that, I like to eat a lot, and I had no desire to change that aspect of my life. Sure, my clothes were tight in some areas, and yes, I had to shop for those elastic bands in the waist but for the most part I was happy. Cheesecake, carrot cake, corn bread, fried potatoes, oh I could go on, and on. The doctor informed me of some blood levels that weren't where they should be and, thus, the experiment began.

Why I call it the experiment is because I felt like that's what I was in! Conversations went something like this: "No fat and no sugar is the best way", and, "Some fat and some sugar is the best way", along with, "Use Splenda instead of sugar. Don't use any artificial sweetener, or they will kill you". It was a nightmare! I couldn't keep up with the ever-changing opinions of all of the so called "experts". However, I knew that I had to do something about it.

Slowly I began eating vegetables (not dipped in batter and fried) and got used to the texture and taste. As a much-needed side note: thank the lord for seasoning. I began to grill, broil, and bake instead of fry, which was a huge change in my overall diet. Water became my go to drink with my occasional diet soda for meals (do not judge me or tell me it will kill me – that's between me and Jesus) and, of course, I had my coffee in the morning.

Here is what happened - CHANGE. My waistline began to shrink, my weight began to drop, my energy level increased, and I started to feel much healthier overall! So, what's the point? So much of our lives are spent going from one extreme to the other. We work too much to make extra money only to miss out on the time spent with friends and family. We spend so much money only to find ourselves in a mountain of debt. We worry too much over things that will still be here long after the stress has killed us.

When we follow Jesus, He places all we need inside of us. Jesus told us this very thing: John 14:26 (ESV) "But the helper the Holy Spirit, whom the Father will send in my name, he will teach you all things and bring to your remembrance all that i have said to you".

His voice still speaks up in the very areas we struggle. He nudges us to pick something up or put it down. We tend to overanalyze things all while taking in everyone else's opinions. He reminds us of what is and isn't good for us. Right now, as you think through your own life, He is stirring and bringing in some of those very things to mind. Lean in sweet sister, listen, then follow.

Question of the Day: What is He bringing to your mind right now that you can change today?

DAY TWENTY – ONE

It's a love thing

Love must be sincere - Romans 12:9 Colossians 3:23-25

Fake it until you make it - we have all heard that before. It sounds like it should work, right? As a Christ follower, I know that we are to love our enemies, pray for those that persecute us, etc. However, how many of us "feel" it? Let me be frank, the last thing I want for my enemies or those that are unkind to me is for them to be blessed!

I would always have the thought, "because I love Jesus, I have to love you, but I don't have to like you!" That is what I stood by. I would try to be kind to the unkind and show compassion, however, I wanted to spit fire on the inside! All the while believing that I was a "good Christian", I would smile when I wanted to scream, laugh when I wanted to cry, and so on.

One day while researching the bible for something completely different, I came across Romans 12:9 and then the standoff began! What do I mean? You know, the deer in the headlight look as I stared at the words - LOVE MUST BE SINCERE. Surely this doesn't mean all the time - surely there is an underlying meaning to break this down. Come on Lord, are you serious right now?

Here is what I came to - He is serious, very serious actually, when it comes to how we love and care for each other. He knows our hearts and knows when we are being real when we aren't. Loving someone that is unkind, unloving, and uncaring from them is something only GOD CAN DO, in which He does through us! Let's face it, there is nothing that is good in us except that's from Him. Jesus even corrected the rich young ruler by answering him, "Why do you call me good? No one is good except God alone" Mark 10:18 (ESV).

So how do we do it (really love others) and it be sincere? We have to stay in constant prayer with Him by asking Him to give us His eyes to see and His ears to hear. Show us a different perspective and give us a new outlook. When He does - it happens! We find ourselves moved with compassion for those that seem cruel. Our hearts will go out to those that hurt others because we realize that it's because the reason they hurt is because they are hurting inside themselves. We do not control how others treat us, however, we do control how we react to it.

Colossians 3:23-25 "Whatever you do, do your work heartily, as for the Lord rather than for men, knowing that from the Lord you will receive the reward of the inheritance. It is the Lord Christ whom you serve. For he who does wrong will receive the consequences of the wrong which he has done, and that without partiality".

Question of the Day: What perspective shift is he trying to get you to see in the very person that drives you crazy?

DAY TWENTY - TWO

Called my Name

I don't know about you but there are times when I would love nothing more than to change my name. I'm sure you have experienced it as well, especially if you have a job or are a parent! Recently I heard for what felt like a solid minute - mama, mama, mama, mama, mama, mama, mama, mama to which I answered with an elevated voice, "WHAT???", to only get the answer of, " I forgot".

If you think about it, our name is always called with the intent of an action statement or question to follow. (Name), did you know or (Name), can you please, etc.

I wonder, if you are anything like me, I can get lost in the "action" or what follows, anticipating what my name was called for!

But that is just it! When our names are called it's because it's our turn. Our turn to listen, our turn for correction, our turn for action. At that moment – it's about us.

Isaiah 43(ESV) says, "But now thus says the Lord he who created you, O Jacob, he who formed you, O Israel: Fear not for I have redeemed you; I have called you by name, you are mine". We have been called by name by God - for what exactly?

We see here in Isaiah our name is called "to Belong", which means we belong to Him! 2 Timothy 1:9 says, "He called us to a Holy Calling", one that is set apart from the world. 1 Peter 2:1 says that we are called to "Follow in His Steps". When God called our names, it wasn't just for salvation, but a ticket to heaven. That in itself is amazing, however, He has work for us to do, which is to follow His example on earth so that others can see Him through us.

I know you've heard the saying: "You may be the only bible anyone will ever read", which is true!

What we "DO" our "Actions" is what the world is looking at. They hear our words, but they "Pay attention" to our actions. Will they back up what we are saying? Here's the crazy thing - He gives us countless times throughout our days to "Be the example".

I know that I hear my name a lot, what about you? Each time I hear my name it resembles a call to action. Once our name is said all eyes are on us; How will we respond to that constant nagging office coworker that drives our skin to crawl? How we handle that diagnosis, the promotion (or lack of one), and how we behave while waiting in a Walmart check-out line, people are always watching. He has called YOUR name! How will you respond?

Question of the day: What type of an example am I being today?

DAY TWENTY - THREE

Wearing a Mask

Halloween has always been one of those holidays where folks go all out to dress up like someone they aren't. It's when that sweet baby girl puts on her princess Elsa dress and sings "Let it go". It's that time of year when that precious little boy puts on the mask of incredible Hulk and gets to be a superhero. However, for so many of us, we wear mask all the time. Never taking them off and if we do it's simply to switch to a different one.

We wear our "Strong" mask- the ones that tell people that we can handle anything, where nothing challenges us and, if it does, we can take control of it in a split second. We wear our "I'm Fine" masks, which say that no matter how our lives are falling apart, and life feels like it's suffocating the air out of our lungs, we are "FINE". I have learned that we sometimes put on masks for all kinds of reasons: the fear of rejection from others or judgement, fear of reality, and fear of the Unknown. If we allowed people to see underneath our masks, how would they treat us? Would the rejection come all at once or in snippets?

I find it interesting that Halloween is a time to wear a mask. It's a time to be spooked and, yet, the reasons listed above for our everyday masks derive from FEAR.

We think that as long as we wear the masks, then no one will see the ONLY way to get closer to our Lord is to remove them all together.

John 8:28 (ESV) states that we will know the truth and the truth will set us free. Staying behind our mask is what the enemy wants, and that is to stay in our sadness, loneliness, and isolation. Jesus called us out into His very light! Paul reminds us in 2 Corinthians that it's in the very weakness we are trying to hide where God's light will shine the brightest! Today is a day to start over!

Time to take off the mask(s) and let Him shine!

Question of the day: What mask(s) are you hiding behind?

DAY TWENTY - FOUR

Words matter

Have you ever heard the old saying, "Sticks and stones will break my bones but words will never hurt me"? I am not sure who came up with that concept but, apparently, they have either lived in a bubble or have never been cut to the core with someone's words.

Words unfortunately do hurt, and they leave a lasting impression. It's been proven that it takes 5 positive comments to overwrite a negative one. One negative remark, and one critical comment can completely rip a person apart.

God's word tells us more than once how powerful our words can be. Proverbs alone can make you stop and take inventory of the ones coming out of our mouths. Proverbs 15:4, "A gentle tongue is a tree of life, but perverseness in it breaks the spirit". Proverbs 16:24, "Gracious words are like honeycomb, sweetness to the soul and helpful to the body". Proverbs 18:4, "The words of a man's mouth are deep waters, the fountain of wisdom is a bubbling brook". See what I mean?

What if we truly gave thought to each word that came out of our mouths? A moment of true "awakening" for me was when Matthew 15:18 popped out of the page in my quiet time with the Lord. That verse says, "but what comes out of the mouth proceeds from the heart, and this defiles a person." So many times, I have let words come out in anger, frustration and aggravation that I would never want to be in my heart. Words that I desperately want to take back but can't because the damage is already done.

To simplify, words do matter. I know that if you are anything like me you have felt them deeper than you'd like to admit, and that they have had some kind of effect on the way you think about things now. Proverbs 18:21 says, "Death and life are in the power of the tongue, and those that love it will eat its fruit". With death and life, we have a choice to speak one or the other. Words of hope, and words of faithfulness.

Instead of focusing on the negatives, why not focus on the positives? Instead of saying, "Today I will never get all that I need to get done," instead say, "Today I will knock things off my list one at a time". Instead of saying, "That person will never change" instead say, "Through God anyone can change!". Instead of saying, "This assignment is ridiculous, I have no idea why we need to do this", instead say, " I am going to look for something good through and in this. I believe God can teach me through anything". To simplify, words bring LIFE!

Question of the day: What words of life can you begin right now to speak over your situation, family or day?

DAY TWENTY - FIVE

Mountaintop

The mountaintop is truly spectacular. However, it doesn't have the same effect unless you go through the climbing process. Many times, we want the mountaintop experience without the hard work to climb, yet, it's in the very climbing that makes the top even sweeter. God has a call on everyone's life.

1 Peter 2:21, "To this you were called because Christ suffered for you, leaving you an example, that you should follow in his steps". Following in the steps of Jesus goes against everything the world tells us to do. It's the extreme opposite!

Think about it, in 1 Peter 3:9 it says, "Don't repay evil for evil. Don't retaliate with insults when people insult you. Instead, pay them back with blessing. That is what God has called you to do, and he will grant you his blessing". From the time, I can remember the words, "if someone hits you, hit them back", following Jesus says to BLESS them! WHAT???

Yet is in that very action that he has a promise. Did you see it? At the end of 1 Peter 3:9 it says, "This is what he has called you to do and He will grant you his blessing". We don't know what that blessing is, however, through scripture we see James 1:17 says that every good and perfect gift is from above. So just because I don't know the "exact" blessing, I am guaranteed that it is good and perfect, which in the end is so much greater than anything the world has to offer. I tend to relate the old mountaintop experience to the old Rocky movies when Rocky fought so hard and he when finally reached the top. His experience clearly showed me that he had to put in the work and go through some rough patches to reach the top of the mountain.

Maybe that is where you feel you are today, which is in a rough patch. My prayer is that you know He is with you always. Isaiah 43:2 says that when we pass through the waters, he will be with us, through the rivers they will not overwhelm us and when we walk through the fire we shall not be burned. Press into the climb - Your mountaintop is almost there!

Question of the day: How can I lean in and look up as I climb today?

DAY TWENTY - SIX

Obedience

Did you know that following Jesus meant following with all we have? Seems simple enough, right? I thought so too until I heard this, "Partial obedience is still disobedience".

I am one of those people that would see a sign that says, "no food or drink", yet would still take a water anyway. Why? Because I have reasoned in my mind that water isn't really in the "drink" category. But here's the thing - Isaiah 55:8 (ESV) says this, "For my thoughts are not your thoughts, neither my ways your ways, declares the Lord".

Am I partially obeying God or am I sold out, giving Him all I got NO MATTER WHAT? Many times, throughout His word we encounter well-meaning people. Those that "love" God, however, seem to only want to follow His direction when and if it's convenient. Take Ananias and Sapphira for example; In Acts 5, we see that they sold land but rather bring all the profits, they only brought part. Then we see Saul who is instructed by the Lord to destroy everything and everyone in 1 Samuel 15. However, Saul only destroys what He thinks has no value and kept what he thought had good.

The Lord will call us to step out and do things that do not make sense and that goes against everything the world has told us is right. We have to be willing to do it no matter what. Peter had been fishing all night long and didn't catch anything. He was washing his nets when Jesus walked up and asked him to go out and lower the nets. Peter's response was golden! He said, "Master, we have toiled all night long and took nothing but at your word I will let down the net". It made no sense to Peter since he had fished all night, however, because Jesus said so he did it anyway! What was the outcome from this? More fish then he could count.

Question of the Day: What is He asking of you that doesn't make sense and you are not following through based on your own reasoning?

DAY TWENTY – SEVEN

The Way

In John 14:6 (ESV) Jesus said to him, "I am the Way, and the Truth, and the LIFE".

When we see the word LIFE, we tend to think to also think of the opposite, death. The moment we give our lives and hearts to Jesus, we realize rather quickly that death no longer has a grip on us.

Paul says in 2 Corinthians 5:8 that absent from the body means we are present with the Lord. We live for eternity with Jesus and although that in itself is such an incredible gift, that isn't all because Jesus has given us so much more.

Anything that we consider, or think is dead, Christ can breathe life into it. Whether that is a broken marriage, a relationship with parent(s), a prodigal child, or an untreatable disease, Christ will be able to breathe life into it.

In Ezekiel 37:1-15, we see that God brought Ezekiel to a valley of dry bones. These bones were beyond hope, because they were laying on the surface of the valley and the sun had dried them out. I don't know about you, but I have had areas that seem hopeless had it not been for our Lord. In the same way those bones began to live exactly the same way He uses our lives today.

Phase one - Bones begin to rattle. Have you ever prayed and heard from the Lord and it seem things shift? Most of the time by baby steps or even it seems they move backwards. Point is - it rattles.

Phase two - skin covers in the same way that the skin covered the bones God is covering us with. That "thing" or "person" you have been praying for or about is covered by prayer of the righteous (you).

James 5:16b (ESV) says, "The prayer of a righteous person has great power as it is working". In other words, your prayer is making a difference!

Phase three: God breaths life, and life comes only from Him. Nothing works no matter how hard we work or pray, but HE IS THE ONE that breaths Life.

Question of the day: What is it in your life today that needs LIFE? How are you covering it in prayer and are you open to what He may ask you to do to move on to the next phase?

DAY TWENTY - EIGHT

Time

As I get older, the realization of time becomes more of a reminder of how quickly it flies and how much control we DO HAVE. For the longest time I allowed bitterness, resentment, anger and, hurt rule my life, which in turn was stealing away any joy and peace that Jesus died to give me.

The front porch of worry is where I would spend 23 out of 24 hours of my day. That was until God began to wake me up! We can reclaim anything in this world: money, cars, homes, food, water, relationships, the list is endless. However, one thing we can NEVER get back is TIME.

We tend to live our lives like one of those sand hourglass timers. Once the sand drains out, we simply turn it over. On the other hand, in reality once the time in our lives falls through that narrow vortex, it's gone never to get back again. A vapor, that's what James calls it in James 4:14, "Appearing for a little while then vanishes away". Yet, Jesus said in John 10:10 that he came to give us life abundant. That means a full life right here on earth.

We tend to shortchange ourselves every moment we waste in any attitude other than thankfulness. Worrying about anything in this life is a waste of His time and our energy, and it doesn't change the situation or circumstance. ALWAYS REMEMBER THAT YOUR CURRENT SITUATION IS NOT YOUR FINAL DESTINATION. Time is short – let's not waste another moment!

Question of the day: How can you be more aware of your time and making the best of what is left?

DAY TWENTY - NINE

In the Know

I've always struggled with being 'nosey'. Now, I normally wouldn't have ever admitted to that. I wanted to disguise it by saying "Intrigued", because that just sounds so much better than "nosey". Yet, they both mean the same thing no matter what word we would use to describe it. That is why social media is so popular, because it gets us in the know.

I was consumed by wanting to know what was going on with everyone around me, so much so that when I tried to disconnect or take a "rest" day I would get this overwhelming feeling that I was being left out. I know, crazy but it's certainly true! God woke me up to something that hit me right in the head (that is exactly how He talks to me most of the time) one day. You see, I didn't need the information if I wasn't planning to use it for God's glory. I didn't need to know that someone's marriage was struggling unless I had planned to seriously pray for them to work it out. I didn't need to know that someone I knew got a promotion unless I was serious about praying for their success.

The enemy loves to get us sidetracked and consumed with everything and everyone other than who and what God has placed right in front of our own eyes. I have learned that if I had to hunt down the information and put forth over the top effort to be involved, then he did not call me to do it. Jesus wants my attention in the now and the person in front of me NOW. He wants the situation in front of me NOW. Sometimes being in the "know" can cause much more stress, anxiety, and worry than if we simply stay in the "NOW".

Question of the day: What information or gossip are you chasing down today that is causing you to miss things He put in front of you? How can you stay in the now today?

DAY THIRTY

Awake

The beach is my place where I can reset. It's the place where I can go and slip easier into a more clear-headed rest. It's in the moments when I feel most close to Him. So much so that I will even get up early (I am not a fan of early) just so I can watch the brilliance of the sun peeking up from over the horizon.

I noticed this past time there were more people out with me than what I had noticed before. Some were on the balconies of their condos, and some even made the extra effort to take a blanket onto the beach shore to watch the magnificence of His handy work. Taking in the sites of those around me took me to a place in Matthew 7:21. Jesus states that not everyone that calls His name Lord, Lord will enter the kingdom.

As I looked over those on the shore, I saw different walks with Jesus. I saw those that like to keep Him in a box, aka, the balcony. I saw those that go the extra mile, for example, blankets and coffee on the shore, those that take others with them on the journey, those sitting with others watching the view, and those walking the edge of the water by themselves.

In order to have a true awakening with God, we must be willing to move forward in whatever state we are in. Being able to expose all of who we are would be allowing Him to take over, and also willing to change and surrender. The key is simple really.

Romans 13:11 (ESV), "Besides this you know the time, that the hour has come for you to wake from sleep. For salvation is nearer to us now than when we first believed". He already knows every detail of our lives and, yet, still chooses us. Every good and bad thing, every thought we have and, yet, he still loves us anyway.

This journey with Him is one that He created which we get to partake in. Not because of the blessings we will gain by the relationship, but rather just by having the relationship itself.

Is He enough? If we lose everyone and everything, is He still enough? If you answer anything other than a resounding YES, then it's time to open up more of your heart and surrender. Only then will you be awakened.

Question of the Day: Am I ready to lose it all for Jesus and Him alone?